D0938866

GIFT OF

*John Warren Stewig*

Carthage

# Tales of Trickery
# from the Land of Spoof

# TALES
# OF TRICKERY
## from the Land of Spoof

COLLECTED AND RETOLD BY

## Alvin Schwartz

PICTURES BY

## David Christiana

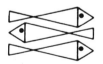

*Farrar, Straus and Giroux*
NEW YORK

Grateful acknowledgment is made to the following for permission
to reprint copyrighted material:

*The American Folklore Society*: "The Dahut" is an adaptation
of the tale "Hunting the Dahut: A French Folk Custom" from the
*Journal of American Folklore* 58(227): 21–24, 1945. Not for further
reproduction.

*Doubleday & Company, Inc.*: "Snouters" adapted from *The
Snouters: Form and Life of the Rhinogrades* by Dr. Harald Stümpke.
Copyright © 1967 by Doubleday & Company, Inc.

*Harcourt Brace Jovanovich, Inc.*: "Footprints on the Ceiling"
adapted from *Abraham Lincoln: The Prairie Years and the War
Years*, one-volume edition by Carl Sandburg, copyright 1926 by
Harcourt Brace Jovanovich, Inc.; renewed 1954 by Carl Sandburg.

*Little, Brown and Company*: "The Magic Turtle" adapted
from *As I Remember Him* by Hans Zinsser. Copyright 1940.

*Harold Matson Company, Inc.*: ". . . and the Shrinking Head,"
"The Organ That Brayed Like a Donkey," "The Case of the Royal
Arabian Jewels," "Alex and Avery," and "The Box Marked
SECRET" adapted from *The Compleat Practical Joker* by H. Allen
Smith, © 1953 by H. Allen Smith. © 1980 by Nelle Smith.

*Charles Scribner's Sons*: "Rattlesnake Soup" excerpted from
*Gone Haywire* by Philip Ashton Rollins. Copyright 1939 Charles
Scribner's Sons; copyright renewed © 1967.

"Billy the Milkmaid" adapted from *Cow by the Tail* by Jesse
James Benton, originally published by Houghton Mifflin Company,
1943.

My thanks to Alan Abel; Earl Coleman of the Princeton University Archive; Rodris Roth and Nancy McLaughlin of the Smithsonian Institution; Barbara C. Schwartz, Peter H. Schwartz, and the librarians at the Princeton, N.J., Public Library, Princeton University, and the University of Maine (Orono) for their help with this book.

ALVIN SCHWARTZ

# Contents

# CONTENTS

# Tales of Trickery
# from the Land of Spoof

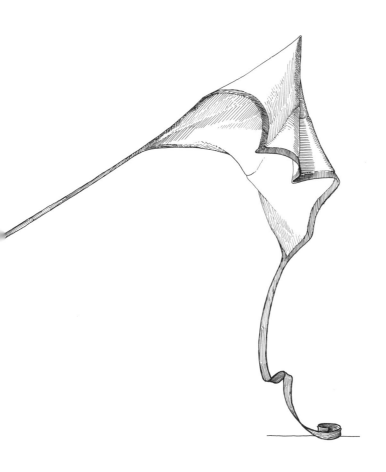

# Bald-Headed Whizzers

**P**EOPLE have been playing tricks on one another for as long as anyone knows. They love to catch their friends off guard and trick them into doing something silly. Then, of course, their friends try to trick them in turn.

Most people get their start in trickery with simple old-fashioned pranks they learn in school or at home or from their friends on April Fools' Day. Most of these tricks are so old they have long white beards. Yet they still are fun and usually they work.

A trickster tells someone that his shoelaces are untied, when they aren't, or that her stocking has a hole in it, when it doesn't.

Or he comes up behind someone who is walking ahead of him. He taps the person on the right shoulder, then totally confuses him or her by passing on the left.

Or he leaves a ring or a purse on the sidewalk with a strong thread attached, then jerks it away when someone tries to pick it up.

For some tricksters, such pranking is only the beginning. Over the years, they move on to tricks that are far more

*(3)*

complicated. One went to great trouble to convince a friend that his head was getting smaller and smaller, when it wasn't. Another created an imaginary college football team that was on its way to an undefeated season. The newspapers not only carried its scores each week but ran articles on its players, when there was no such team or school.

For even a simple trick to work, a trickster must be cool, and that comes with practice. If he is sure of himself, it is not hard to trick someone. But if he giggles or fools around or appears nervous, he may give the joke away.

When the American West was being settled, people played so many tricks on one another that they began to give them ratings. A good trick that was worth repeating was called a "whizzer." The very best tricks were "bald-headed whizzers." Those are the ones you must watch for. When you least expect it, one of them will be waiting for you.

# The Magic Turtle

THE candy store was owned by Madame Perrier and her husband, Louis. They lived in an apartment above the store with six goldfish and a small turtle no more than an inch across.

Madame kept the fish and the turtle in a fish tank on a sill outside the kitchen window. Several times a day, she fed them bread crumbs and talked to them about the weather, the store, the candy, whatever was on her mind.

A college student named Jack lived in the apartment just above the Perriers. On warm spring nights, he would lean out his open window and watch Madame feed her pets, and eavesdrop as she talked to them.

One evening, as he was watching and listening, he had an idea. It seemed so silly that he laughed. But then he thought, Madame would not mind. She would think it was funny.

The next day, Jack bought five turtles at a pet shop. They all looked just like Madame Perrier's turtle, except that they were larger. They ranged in size from about two inches across to about six inches across. He also bought some cheesecloth and wire and a bamboo fishing pole.

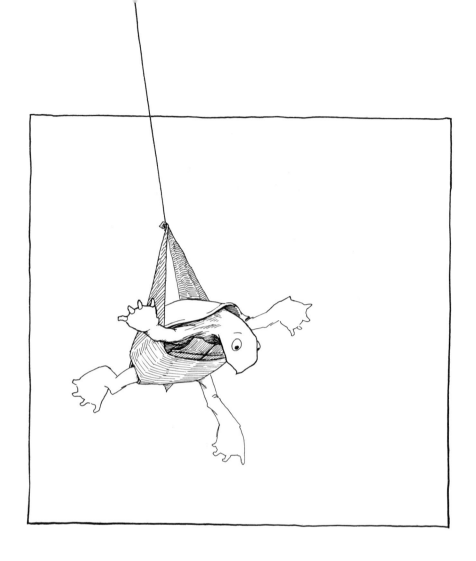

That night, Jack made a small scoop net with the cheese-cloth and wire and attached it to the fishing pole. Early the next morning, before anyone else was awake, he reached out of his kitchen window with the scoop net and removed Madame's turtle from the tank. He put it in a bucket of water. Then he replaced it with a turtle that was two inches across or twice as large.

When Madame saw the turtle, she got very excited. "It's

*twice* as big as it was yesterday!" she told Louis. The next morning, Jack removed the two-inch turtle and replaced it with a four-inch turtle. It had doubled in size again! When Madame saw it, she ran to the telephone and called everybody she knew.

The following morning, while the Perriers slept, Jack removed the four-inch turtle and replaced it with a turtle that was five inches across. *That* caused a sensation. All day long, people in the neighborhood came to see the magic turtle, then went out and told others. The crowd got so large a policeman was sent to keep order. Soon a reporter arrived to interview Madame and take her picture with the turtle. Madame was going to be famous!

Jack decided not to replace the five-inch turtle with his six-inch turtle. The tank did not seem large enough. He also was afraid that Madame could not stand the shock. Instead, he decided to make the turtle smaller once more.

Early the next morning, Jack replaced the five-inch turtle with a three-inch turtle. Of course, when Madame discovered what had happened, the excitement continued. Still more people came to see the turtle, and the reporter came back to interview her again.

The next morning, Jack replaced the three-inch turtle with the one-inch turtle Madame owned at the beginning. That night, he put away the dip net and the bamboo pole. He took his five turtles to the park and let them loose in a stream. On the way home, he stopped in to see Madame's turtle. It was away for a while, at the zoo, she said. A scientist was studying its strange behavior.

# ... and the Shrinking Head

WHILE on a visit to London, an American lawyer bought a hat of which he was very proud. When he returned home, he wore the hat to his office every day and talked about it a great deal. Soon his law partners decided that they had heard enough of this hat. They came up with a scheme to stop his endless talk.

They sent to England for four more hats exactly like the one he had bought. They were the same color and the same style. And each had their partner's initials stamped on the inside, just as they were on his own hat. There was only one difference. All the hats they bought were larger than his. His hat was a size 7. Theirs were sizes $7\frac{1}{4}$, $7\frac{1}{2}$, $7\frac{3}{4}$, and 8.

After the lawyer arrived in the office each morning, his partners managed to replace his hat with a new hat in the next size. The first day, they replaced it with size $7\frac{1}{4}$. When he got ready to go out to lunch and put it on, it felt a little loose, but he didn't pay any attention.

The second day, they substituted size $7\frac{1}{2}$. When the lawyer put it on later that day, it seemed too large. Thinking it might be someone else's hat, he took it off and examined it.

It was the same color, had the same initials, and came from the same store. It clearly was his. He did not understand why it did not fit properly any longer. He wondered if his head was shrinking. He felt it with his hands, then he examined it in a mirror. But he didn't see anything to be concerned about. So he put the hat back on and tried not to think about it.

The third day, his partners substituted size 7¾. When he put his hat on later in the day, he became even more concerned. The hat was much too large. He checked the color again, and the initials, and the store. It was his hat. His head *must* be shrinking. What else could it be? He asked his partners what they thought. Had they ever heard of such a thing? Never, they said.

The fourth day, they substituted size 8. When he put the hat on, it seemed larger than ever. He called his doctor and talked to him about it. "It can't be anything serious," his doctor said, but the lawyer made an appointment with him, just in case ...

There also is the story of a fellow who used a cane and was tricked in a similar way. Each day, one of his friends sawed off an eighth of an inch from the bottom of the cane. As the cane grew shorter and shorter, the man began to believe that he was growing taller and taller ...

# Onions

IN the years before the American Revolution, an American officer made a British officer very angry. Just what the American did is not known, but the British officer sent him a letter challenging him to a duel with pistols.

When he did not get a reply, the Englishman went to the American's tent. He found him there, sitting on a wooden powder keg, quietly smoking his pipe.

"Why haven't you answered my letter?" the Englishman demanded.

"Why, you see," said the American, "I am but a poor miserable Yankee that never fired a pistol in my life. If I agree to fight with pistols, you would have an unfair advantage.

"But I do have another suggestion. I have here two powder kegs. I have bored a hole in each one and I have inserted a slow fuse in each hole. If you sit on that keg, I will continue to sit on this one. I will then light both fuses. The one who dares to sit the longest on his keg shall be called the bravest fellow and will win the duel."

The Englishman agreed, and the American lighted the fuses. Then they both sat on their kegs. The American sat calmly smoking his pipe. But the English officer was very nervous. When the fuses had burned to within an inch of the kegs, he leaped to his feet and dashed away. What the American had not told him was that the powder kegs now were filled with onions.

# Rattlesnake Soup

**F**OR a meal you will never forget, try some thick, chunky rattlesnake soup, brimming over with big juicy pieces of freshly killed rattlesnake. It's a lot of trouble to make, but it's worth it.

(*13*)

You will need a gallon-size bucket and a quart-size can, the kind tomatoes come in. The bucket should be slightly rusty on the inside, to add the right amount of iron to the soup. Just be sure the rust doesn't go all the way through, or the soup will leak out.

You also will need about a dozen young, tender rattlesnakes and about a dozen older ones with a stronger flavor. Cut off the heads of the snakes just behind the ear slits, and store them in the quart can. Cover them with cold water to keep them nice and fresh. Then remove the rattles and set them aside.

Next, cover the bottom of the bucket with young, tender sagebrush leaves and a prickly pear cut up fine. Cut the snakes crosswise into pieces about three inches long. Place them in layers on top of the sagebrush. The first layer should be crosswise, the second lengthwise, and so on, until you use up all the snake meat. Some folks like to cut the snakes into long thin strips, like spaghetti noodles, but that gives you a stringy soup instead of a chunky soup.

Now, add some blackstrap molasses, a few drops of vinegar, and as much salt, red pepper, black pepper, and mustard as you like. Mix it up with a big stick. For a decoration, put the heads on top, sort of looking up at you, and the rattles in a circle around them. That should look mighty pretty.

Then get on your horse and out of there as fast as you can, and leave the whole stinkin' mess behind.

# Johnny Chung and the
# Flying Figments

I N its first game of the football season, Plainfield Teachers College of New Jersey smashed Benson Institute 20–0. Under the leadership of its Chinese-American superstar, Johnny Chung, the team went on to beat the next six schools it played. With only two more games, it was on its way to an undefeated, untied season.

Although Plainfield was a small school, the Flying Figments, as they were known, were getting a lot of attention in the New York newspapers. Of course, Johnny Chung had a lot to do with that.

Nicknamed the "Celestial Comet," Chung had gained an average of 7.9 yards per carry in the first seven games. He had scored more than half of the Figments' points. When he didn't carry the ball himself, he threw touchdown passes to his partner, "Boarding House" Smithers. According to some reports, he ate bowls of steaming brown rice at half-time to keep up his unusual strength.

With the season almost over, the Plainfield football team had only one problem it could not solve. It did not exist. It was a figment of the imagination of a Wall Street stockbroker named Morris Newburger.

Newburger had wondered why there wasn't more news about small college football teams in the newspapers. Then, one Saturday night, he had an idea. He called the Sports Department at *The New York Times*.

"I wish to report," he said, "that the Plainfield, New Jersey, Teachers College defeated Winona today 27–3."

"Thanks," said a voice at the other end.

Newburger then called the New York *Herald Tribune*, which still was being published in those days, and gave them the same information.

The next morning, both newspapers carried the score. It was hard for Newburger to believe, but it had been as easy as pie. Then Newburger thought, Why not create a whole season?

With the help of some other stockbrokers, he did just that. They first invented a coach they named Ralph "Hurry-Up" Hobitzel, then a roster of imaginary players, with Morris Newburger at quarterback, and his relatives and friends at other positions. Of course, Johnny Chung was at halfback, and "Boarding House" Smithers was at one of the ends.

Next, they worked out a schedule of games their team would play against other imaginary teams. Since the real season was half gone, they made believe that Plainfield already had played and beaten several of their opponents.

Finally, they created a publicity man for the team. They named him Jerry Croyden. They had a press release printed with his name on it and installed a telephone where he could be reached in Morris Newburger's office. Each week, Croyden (played by Newburger and others) called in the score of the latest Plainfield victory and sent out news releases on the players.

The week after Plainfield beat Winona, the team crushed Randolph Tech 35–0. Then they went on to beat Ingersoll 13–0.

Someone who knew about the prank thought it was so funny that he told someone else, and that person told another. Soon a reporter at *Time* magazine heard about it and wrote a story that exposed the hoax.

Newburger asked *Time* not to print the story until the end of the season, but the magazine could not do that. It had to print the truth, it explained. So Jerry Croyden sent out his final news release. It said that Plainfield had called off its last two games. The reason was that several players, including Johnny Chung, had failed their midterm examinations. It was too bad, because Plainfield would have won both of them.

# The Organ That Brayed Like a Donkey

AN organist was giving a concert, but he could not get the pipe organ to work properly. He would press down on a key, and the organ would bray like a donkey. Finally, he threw up his hands in despair, walked to the side of the stage, and called to some workmen who happened to be waiting in the wings.

While the audience watched, the workmen examined the organ. They had started to take down the largest of the organ pipes when they dropped it. The pipe broke in half, and out flew a flock of chickens, ducks, pigeons, and other birds. The workmen carted away the broken organ and as many of the birds as they could catch. Then the organist went back to his concert.

None of this was an accident. It was all Hugh Troy's doing. Later, Troy became a well-known painter of murals. But in those days he was a student at Cornell University in Ithaca, New York, and was just getting his start as a trickster. The

pipe-organ prank was only one of many that he played while he was there.

One time, he borrowed an unusual wastepaper basket that had been made from the hollowed-out foot of a rhinoceros. After a snowfall, he and a friend filled the foot with some heavy pieces of scrap metal, to give it more weight. Then they attached a clothesline to each side and started walking it across the campus, leaving behind a long trail of rhino tracks.

When someone followed the big tracks the next day, they took him out to the middle of a frozen lake. There they disappeared at the edge of a big hole in the ice, as if whatever it was had fallen through and drowned. Since the university depended on the lake for drinking water, the tracks and the hole attracted a lot of attention.

After some experts said the tracks were those of a rhinoceros, students insisted that the drinking water now had the flavor of a rhino, whatever that is like. Only when they realized that it was a joke did the water again taste the way it always had.

Another time, Hugh borrowed a pair of rubbers from a professor and painted them to look like white feet. Then he covered the painted feet with lampblack. The next time the professor wore the rubbers in the rain, the lampblack washed off. He looked as if he was walking around in his bare feet.

Hugh had a professor who complained constantly about the ceiling in his classroom. He was afraid it was going to fall down and was forever demanding that something be done about it. One night, Hugh and some friends hauled a ladder into the room and painted what looked like a big, black hole in the ceiling. On the floor directly under the "hole," they left a big pile of broken plaster.

When the professor arrived in class early the next morning, he took one quick look at the mess, shouted "Aha!" and raced off to complain once again. While he was gone, Hugh and his friends quickly painted out the black hole and hauled off the debris. By the time the professor returned with a crew to make repairs, the hole was gone and everything was back to normal.

Hugh helped to pay for his expenses in college by working for the university's athletic department. His job was to send to newspapers throughout the state the results of the track meets in which Cornell competed. For each event, he would list the names of the students in the order in which they finished, along with their time.

It soon occurred to him that these reports must be very embarrassing to the students who finished last in an event. So he invented a new member of the track team, a student he named Johnny Tsal. Tsal was slower than all the others, and he always finished last. As a result, no one else ever did.

# The Case of the
# Royal Arabian Jewels

**W**HEN a trickster named Jim Moran learned that the crown prince of Saudi Arabia was in Hollywood for a long visit, he decided to pose as the prince one night and see what it was like to be treated as royalty.

He would wait until the prince was out of town for a while, then dress in Arab robes and have dinner in a fancy restaurant. But that was only part of his plan.

He hired three actors to help him, one to pose as his Arab dinner companion, the other two as his servants. He arranged with a costume company to rent the robes and other clothing they would need. Then he bought a big batch of glass "jewels." He also bought a large amethyst, an inexpensive gemstone that looks more valuable than it is. He stored his "jewels" in a large leather pouch.

When Moran heard that the prince had left Hollywood for a few days, he called an expensive restaurant that was popular with movie stars and reserved a table for that night. He also rented a chauffeur-driven limousine. After Moran

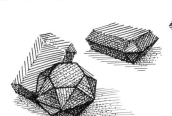

and the three actors dressed in their costumes, the limousine took them to dinner.

When they arrived at the restaurant, the two servants went inside to make certain that the table was suitable for the prince. Then they brought in the prince and his friend. After they seated them, they stood nearby.

Their table was at the edge of the dance floor. Whenever the dance band played, the dancers jostled one another to get a good look at the royal party. Moran ignored them. But at one point he sent one of the servants to ask the band leader to play "Begin the Beguine," a popular song that was one of his favorites.

After the band played the song, the prince smiled at the band leader and nodded his approval. Then he pulled out his pouch of "jewels" and emptied it on the tablecloth. As everyone in the restaurant watched, he selected the amethyst. He examined it in the light, then sent it to the band leader as a token of his appreciation.

Soon after dinner, the prince decided to leave. Since there was no one dancing, his party started across the dance floor toward the door. Suddenly the prince's jewel pouch opened, and the glass "jewels" it held fell to the floor, spilling in all directions.

The servants started to pick them up, but the prince shrugged his shoulders. "Leave them," he said, and swept from the room without looking back.

As the Arabs were seating themselves in the limousine, everyone in the restaurant was on hands and knees scrambling for the "jewels" the prince had left behind.

# Footprints on the Ceiling

WHEN Abe Lincoln was a teenager, he got some young boys to go wading in a mud puddle near his home. After they got their feet good and muddy, he picked up the boys one at a time and carried them inside. There he turned them upside down. Then, holding them tightly, he got them to walk their muddy feet across the ceiling, leaving a trail of black footprints where no one ever would expect to see them.

# "A Nude Horse Is a Rude Horse"

ONCE there was a man named G. Clifford Prout who believed that dogs, cats, horses, cows, and other domestic animals should wear clothing. "Nude animals are indecent," he said. "They are a cause of low moral standards and juvenile delinquency."

Prout believed this so strongly that he formed an organization to work toward dressing all domestic animals in shirts, pants, skirts, shorts, or similar clothing. He called it the Society for Indecency to Animals, or SINA, for short.*

SINA's goal was to have every domestic animal over four inches tall and six inches long wear clothing. Prout's own horse, Wings of Destiny, wore brightly colored walking shorts. "A nude horse is a rude horse," Mr. Prout often said.

For many years, Prout had tried to talk to animals and communicate with them in other ways. He was certain this

*Prout actually meant the "Society for Decency to Animals," but he never got around to correcting his mistake.

was possible, but he never succeeded. The reason, he decided, was the shame the animals felt at having to appear in the nude.

"Look closely at a herd of cattle who seem to be grazing," he said. "You will find that they are not grazing at all. They are just hanging their heads in shame."

Prout was a wealthy St. Louis businessman. When he died, he left his son, G. Clifford Jr., $400,000 to carry on his crusade. The first thing that G. Clifford Jr. did was set up a headquarters for SINA on Fifth Avenue in New York. Then he began traveling to spread his father's beliefs. He went from place to place, making speeches, giving interviews, and organizing demonstrations to show the need to clothe the animals.

In San Francisco, G. Clifford Jr. visited the zoo, where he dressed a goat in knickers, a burro in bloomers, and a fawn in a bikini. He also toured pet shops and humane societies in the city. He estimated that there were 463,000 naked animals in San Francisco and called the city "a moral disaster area." After his visit, the *San Francisco Chronicle* ran a banner headline which read: SF CENTER OF WAR ON NAKED ANIMALS.

When John F. Kennedy was President, G. Clifford Jr. picketed the White House, carrying signs that scolded Mrs. Kennedy for allowing her children to ride naked horses.

To help people dress their animals, SINA distributed free clothing patterns for dog, cat, cow, horse, and goat clothing. It also operated fourteen SINA "clothesmobiles," with drivers trained to locate nude animals and quickly dress them.

*(28)*

## "A Nude Horse Is a Rude Horse"

SINA was such an unusual organization that articles about it appeared in many magazines and newspapers. G. Clifford Jr. was on the NBC Today show twice, and on other talk shows as well. He also was interviewed on the CBS Evening News. He finished that interview by singing "The Wings of Destiny," the official SINA marching song, while playing the ukulele. These are the lyrics:

*High on the wings of SINA*
*Fight for the future now.*
*Let's clothe every pet and animal*
*Whether dog, cat, horse, or cow.*
*G. Clifford Prout, our president,*
*He works for you and me.*
*So clothe all your pets and join the march*
*For worldwide de-cen-cy.*

As a result of all this publicity, SINA headquarters in New York was flooded with letters and telephone calls. Many people wanted to join. Some wanted to start SINA chapters. Some sent money to help pay for SINA's work. Some sent snapshots of animals that were now wearing clothes. There were others who wrote to say that G. Clifford Jr. was crazy or was part of a plot to overthrow the United States.

What was amazing about all this is that so many people believed there was an organization called SINA when there wasn't. SINA, Prout, and G. Clifford Jr. were all part of a hoax by an advertising man named Alan Abel. Abel got the idea one morning as he waited in a line of cars for some cattle to cross the road outside Denton, Texas.

As the cattle slowly made their way across, a cow and a
bull stopped and made love. The way in which people in the
other cars reacted caught Abel's attention. They all seemed
to be embarrassed. One woman put her fingers in her ears,

closed her eyes, and placed her head on the steering wheel. The others simply looked away.

As Abel watched the cattle and the people, he decided to write a short story in which a man named G. Clifford Prout starts a crusade against naked animals. But none of the magazines he contacted was interested.

One morning several years later, however, Abel happened to tune in to NBC's Today show, and had another idea. Why not use the story of G. Clifford Prout to show how silly people can be? He turned off the TV set and wrote a letter to Today, describing how naked animals lowered our moral standards. He said that he was president of SINA, and asked that they interview him about this important issue. He signed the letter G. Clifford Prout, Jr.

To Abel's surprise, the Today show was interested in interviewing G. Clifford Prout, Jr. Since there was no such person, Abel hired an actor named Buck Henry to pretend that he was G. Clifford Jr.

One day several weeks later, millions of people eating their breakfasts watched as G. Clifford told them about SINA and the need to get their animals dressed. As examples of what he had in mind, he showed drawings of a cat in overalls, a cow in a sort of wraparound skirt, and a horse in walking shorts (his father's horse, Wings of Destiny). No one realized that SINA was a hoax, least of all the show's staff. In fact, G. Clifford Jr. was invited back for a second visit.

Buck Henry's appearance on the Today show, and on other talk shows, stirred up a lot of interest in SINA, so much that Alan Abel decided to continue the hoax for a while longer. He was having too much fun to stop just yet.

Abel had leaflets about SINA printed; he obtained a telephone number for the organization and hired an answering service to handle all the telephone calls coming in. To give SINA an impressive address, he rented a broom closet in an office building on Fifth Avenue in New York. He had *Society for Indecency to Animals* lettered on the door.

A receptionist told visitors that everyone at the office was out of town. But Abel figured that someone would try to look through the keyhole. So he left a light on and a picture on the wall of Prout's horse in gaily colored walking shorts.

Interest in SINA continued to grow. Over forty thousand people became members. Soon, news reporters began to wonder whether such a strange organization was legitimate. With a little research, they learned what we know. Soon, stories appeared in both *Time* and *Newsweek* telling the truth about SINA.

But it didn't seem to matter. Many people continued to believe that SINA was a real organization and that dressing animals in skirts, pants, and overalls was a good idea. When this was written, twenty-five years after the hoax got started, the SINA telephone number still was listed in the New York telephone directory, and every week as many as a dozen calls and letters still were coming in.

# Getting Older and Older
# Faster and Faster

**H**ERE is a puzzle.

Suppose that a man is thirty years old and that he has a daughter who is one year old. He is *thirty times* older than his daughter.

But when that child is thirty years old, the father will be sixty, or only *twice* as old as she is.

And when his daughter is sixty, he will be ninety, or only *one-third* older than she is.

If she lives to be ninety and her father is still alive, he would be one hundred and twenty, or only *one-fourth* older than his child.

As you can see, she has been growing older at a faster rate than her father, and is gradually gaining on him. It seems that, at some point, she must overtake him. Suppose that both live long enough for this to happen. How old would they be when the daughter finally is older than her father?

The solution is on page 77, in the note "Getting Older."

# The Dahut

WHEN Joe was fourteen years old, he spent part of his summer vacation at his uncle's house in the country. One day, he came across a curious sign at the edge of a small woods. The sign read:

DAHUT HUNTING IS FORBIDDEN!

Since Joe dreamed of becoming a hunter someday, the sign was of great interest to him. He had never heard of a dahut. But when he asked what kind of an animal it was, no one would tell him. Instead, they would say something along these lines: "It is an animal boys of your age do not hunt. You are too young. Maybe next year." No matter whom he asked, that was always the answer.

When Joe visited his uncle the following summer, he had with him his friend Robert. He told his uncle that he and Robert wanted to hunt the dahut. His uncle agreed to help them.

"The dahut is not seen too often," his uncle said. "It is found only here and there, usually on a mountain or a hillside. It has strange legs. They are longer on the right than on the left. That is what keeps it from falling off a steep place."

(34)

He was silent for a minute. Then he said, "We will try to find a dahut for you tomorrow night. When it is dark, they are easier to find."

The next night, Joe's uncle gave each of the boys an empty sack and a lantern. "When we find a good place," he said, "you must set the lantern on the ground, stand behind it with the sack wide open, and wait. But be patient; it can take quite a while.

"While you are waiting, the rest of us go off into the woods," he added. "By beating on pots and pans, we try to drive the dahut toward you. When it sees the light, it will race toward the lantern, then jump into your sack. The minute that happens, tie up the sack as fast as you can. Otherwise, the dahut may escape and turn on you."

When they set out for the woods, Joe's uncle led the way, followed by Joe and Robert. Then came several beaters carrying pots and pans and big spoons with which to bang them. They hiked along an old, badly rutted road overgrown with roots, brambles, and the limbs of overhanging trees.

When they finally reached the woods, Joe's uncle told the boys that they must remain silent, or they would drive away any dahuts that might be there. He pointed to a place where Joe was to stand and to another, thirty yards away, for Robert. They quickly set out their lanterns, opened their sacks, and waited for a dahut.

Meanwhile, Joe's uncle led the beaters into the woods, where they went about banging on their pots and pans, trying to stir up the dahuts.

Joe and Robert waited and waited in the hazy darkness.

Soon, the sounds of the beaters began to fade. After a while, it seemed to Joe that no one was in the woods but Robert and him. They stood watching, listening, waiting for a telltale movement or sound. But all they heard were leaves rustling in the wind, and all they saw were trees and the weird shadows they cast in the lantern light.

As time crept by, the shadows of the trees seemed more and more to Joe like ghosts moving about, and arms and claws reaching out...

A screech owl brushed against Joe's face and screamed. Joe dropped his sack and ran. He shouted to Robert, and the two dashed through the woods to the old rutted road. They ran down the road as fast as they could, tripping and falling, tearing their clothes, and cutting their hands and faces.

When they finally got home, almost everybody in the village was waiting for them. A great shout of laughter went up when the crowd saw the two boys. But when Joe's uncle called them "great hunters of the dahut," there were cheers. From then on, Joe and Robert were beaters. Never again were they hunters left to hold the sack.

This dahut hunt took place in France. The trick also is played in the United States and Canada, but there the victim waits for a snipe instead of a dahut.

# The Wonderful Horse

"**S**EE the wonderful horse!" the carnival man called. "Its head is where its tail should be!"

Each time somebody bought a ticket, the man took the customer into the tent to see it. But all he saw was an ordinary horse standing in an ordinary stall.

Usually, a horse stands with its head at the front of a stall, so that it can see what is going on. But this horse had its

tail in front, where its head should be, and its head in back, where its tail belonged, just as the man had said.

When the customer realized that he had been tricked, and in the silliest way, he could not help but laugh. "Better not tell your friends," the man said, "or you'll never hear the end of it."

So when the customer came out of the tent, and his friends asked him about the horse, he urged them to go and see it. "It's just like the carnival man said," he told them. "You'll never forget it."

And after they had seen it, they urged their friends to see it, too. And those friends told still others. And so it went, each tricking his friends in turn. It is said that no one has ever given this secret away.

# Alex and Avery

ERIC Carson and his wife, Gloria, lived in an apartment in New York City with their big sheep dogs, Alex and Avery. Gloria took the dogs to the park twice a day, at eleven in the morning and at three in the afternoon. There they could run and get the exercise they needed.

When Gloria had to spend a week away from home, she asked Eric to take the dogs to the park every day, as she did. Eric agreed, but leaving his office twice a day interfered with his work. He wondered if there was not another way to give Alex and Avery their exercise.

Eric then recalled that the dogs would race back and forth in the apartment whenever the telephone rang. Instead of leaving his office, he decided to call home twice a day at the appointed hour. He would let the telephone ring for ten or fifteen minutes at eleven and at three and give the dogs their exercise that way.

He would listen for a few minutes to be sure he had not dialed a wrong number. Then he would set the phone aside while it rang and continue his work.

Eric was so proud of his solution that he told all his

friends about it. But he talked about it so much they soon
became tired of the story. Soon, one of them managed to get
a key to Eric's apartment and let himself in just before Eric
made his afternoon call.

Promptly at three, the telephone began to ring, and Alex
and Avery began to race back and forth. Soon after the phone
started ringing, Eric's friend picked it up. He held the speaker
close to his mouth and panted into it the way a big sheep dog
does after it has been running.

"Huh! Huh! Huh!" he went.

Then he hung up.

# Billy the Milkmaid

WHEN I first got out to Arizona in the old days, I landed near Wilcox, where there was a lot of gold and silver mining going on. I took my meals at a boarding house run by a lady named Mrs. Lemons.

Mrs. Lemons was feeding about a hundred miners a day. They were always asking for milk to drink, but she never had enough for them. So it occurred to me that I might go into the milk business and supply her with the milk she needed. We talked it over and worked out an agreement.

"I'll try to get a herd of cows together this week," I told her. Since there weren't any large milk herds in Arizona back then, I had to get my cows and calves one or two at a time from small farmers. I got most of them about fifty miles to the west, where quite a few Mormons were farming.

I started building corrals and sheds and bought a lot of milk pails. Soon, I was ready to begin, but my cows weren't. Some would give only a pint of milk at a time, some just a quart, some nothin' at all. When I'd try to get more, they'd start kicking, and sometimes I'd get kicked into the fence.

I was sure that those Mormon farmers had lied to me

about these being milk cows. I was telling somebody about it when this old Mormon miner came up to me.

"Say, pardner," he said, "them cows you bought were bein' milked by wimmin folks. Don't you know that a Mormon man never does the milkin'?

"See my lip?" he said. It was all gouged and crooked. "That's from a kick I got one night when I tried to do some milkin'. Put a dress on tonight when you go out, and you won't have no trouble."

Well, I talked to Mrs. Lemons. I said I wanted to hire some of the girls who were waitin' table for her to milk my cows. But she said they were all city girls from Kansas City and didn't know anything about cows. So that wouldn't work.

When I told her what the old miner had said, she offered to lend me a dress to wear, and I accepted. "You and me are about the same size," I said. (I told her that to please her. She weighed over two hundred pounds, and I was only a hundred and sixty-five myself.) So she brung out a red calico dress and a sunbonnet. To tell the truth, it was a mighty pretty outfit.

Well, the next morning I shaved off my beard and my mustache and went down to the corral and put on the dress. It was a perfect fit, after I tucked it in here and there and tied a string around the waist. Then I put on the sunbonnet, got some milk pails, and went down to see the cows.

Well, those cows took one look at me and they relaxed. When they knew a woman was at the controls, they stopped kicking and started giving milk the way they were supposed

to. But, gettin' rigged up that way, it turned out I fooled more than just the cows.

I was out there milkin', dressed up like a woman, when along come a bunch of miners on their way home from work. They stopped and stared at me. What a surprise! A new dairy in town and a fine young lady for a milkmaid. "Howdy, lady!" they'd call out, and I'd nod my head and smile, but didn't say a word. Soon, another bunch would come by, and we would go through the same thing.

In a couple of days, they all began comin' back for milk. "Lady, do you have any milk to sell?" they'd ask.

"Yes, sir, plenty," I answered, speaking in a tiny little voice that I tried to make sweet and ladylike.

For a change, everything was going fine. The cows were behaving like cows, I was selling a lot of milk, and I had three dates for that night. Three of the miners had asked me out.

Around eight o'clock, one of them, then another, came to the boarding house and asked for the new milkmaid. The boy who worked for me told them I had gone to town, which was true as far as it went. Of course, I wasn't wearing my dress or sunbonnet, just my regular clothes.

Then they come to town lookin' for me, each one separate, not knowin' about the others. Some of the boys and I were watching, and it sure was funny to see them fellers looking up and down the streets, and waiting on corners for me to show up, and there I was, just fifty feet away.

# Pierre Brassau

A N art gallery in Göteborg, Sweden, had some paintings for sale by an unknown artist named Pierre Brassau. Brassau's paintings did not have subjects that were easy to recognize. Each was a wild arrangement of bright colors that looked as if it had been thrown at the canvas. The use of colors in this way is sometimes called "non-objective" painting.

An art critic for one of the city's newspapers was impressed with Brassau's work. He praised the furious twists and turns of the brush strokes and also the delicacy of some of the painting. "Brassau paints with the delicacy of a ballet dancer," the critic wrote.

But another critic thought Brassau's paintings were crude and disgusting. "Only an ape could paint such pictures," he said. This critic was closer to the truth than he knew. Brassau was not an ape. But he was a chimpanzee named Peter.

Peter became involved when some newspaper reporters were sitting around one night in Göteborg and had a disagreement over non-objective painting. Some said it was an important form of art. Others claimed it was no better than finger painting. Even a monkey could do it, they said.

To prove this, they went to one of the keepers at the local zoo. For a bribe, he agreed to give Peter some oil paints, a paintbrush, and a few canvases to paint on.

When Peter first was given his paints, he didn't know what they were, and he ate a whole tube of cobalt blue. But after he ripped open another tube, he somehow got the idea and began painting. He painted all over the floor of his cage, using his paws as well as the brush. Then he painted all over his keeper. When the canvases got in his way, he painted all over them.

Peter's paintings were taken to the art gallery, where they were framed and displayed as the work of Pierre Brassau. Soon, somebody bought one for ninety dollars.

# Snouters

WHAT follows is from a small book called *The Snouters*, by Professor Dr. Harald Stümpke, more of whom you will learn shortly.

These snouters about which Stümpke wrote were no ordinary creatures. Some stood on their noses. Others walked on their noses. Still others had noses that looked like flowers. One species used its ears to fly and its nose to steer and land. And there were others who used their noses, or snouts, in different ways.

The snouters were discovered by chance in 1941 during the Second World War. A Swedish citizen named Einar Petterssen-Skämtkvist escaped in a small boat from a Japanese prisoner-of-war camp. After drifting for several days, his boat was wrecked on a coral reef off the island of Hiduddify in the Hy-yi-yi Islands, which then were unknown to the outside world.

When the natives of these islands, the Hooakha-Hutchi, brought him ashore, Petterssen-Skämtkvist was suffering from a bad cold. Until then, it was an illness that did not exist on Hiduddify and the natives had no natural defenses against it.

As a result, when they caught his cold, they died. In a matter of a few months, all the Hooakha-Hutchi were wiped out by the cold germs.

Petterssen-Skämtkvist lived alone on Hiduddify until he was rescued in 1945 after the war ended. As he explored the island during those years, he came upon colonies of small cuddly animals with very strange noses. These were, of course, snouters.

When he returned to Sweden, he told his friend Harald Stümpke about them. Stümpke was a university zoologist, but he had never heard of such creatures, nor had the zoologists with whom he worked. As soon as he could, he traveled to Hiduddify to see them for himself.

He was so excited by the snouters he saw that he moved to the island to study them. Soon, he founded a center for snouter research that he called the Darwin Institute, and he brought along other researchers to work with him.

During the next few years, they identified 189 separate species whose noses had developed in different ways. Described here are just a few of those they found.

EARWING SNOUTER (*Otopteryx volitans*). This snouter used its large muscular ears to fly backward. It used its slender, graceful snout to steer and land. The colors of its pelt were constantly changing with the light. As it darted about, it reminded Stümpke of a hummingbird or a tropical butterfly.

To launch itself into the sky, the earwing raised its ears to a vertical position, flexed its snout, and jumped off the

ground backward. While it was moving upward, it extended its snout (see sketch) and lowered its earwings. Then it raised them and lowered them faster and faster until it reached ten wingbeats per second and was airborne.

When it wished to land, it glided back to earth, with its nose in landing position.

MIRACULOUS FLOWER-FACED SNOUTER (*Corbulonasus longicauda*). This species was among the most beautiful of the snouters. Its snout was shaped just like a flower. Both its head and its snout were supported by its very long tail, in the same way that a real flower is supported by its stem. It lived in meadows with thousands of other flower-faced snouters, each the color of the snouter nearest to it.

Since the flower-faced snouter could not move away, it relied on the odor of buttermilk it gave off to attract the insects it fed on. When they settled on the edge of its flower-shaped snout, its petals snapped shut, and it sucked them into its mouth. These snouters mated on windy days, when males and females were blown together.

MORGENSTERN'S NASOBAME (*Nasobema lyricum*). Many snouters had four or more snouts they used for walking and leaping. Of these, Morgenstern's Nasobame was the largest, growing to a height of three feet.

To reach the fruit it ate, the Morgenstern depended on its unusually long tail. When fully extended, the tail was four yards long. When the snouter saw what it wanted, it hurled its tail into the fruit tree and pulled it down. When it came to a river or a ravine too wide to cross on its snouts, it wrapped its tail around a high branch in a tree and swung across.

The Morgenstern had only one enemy. It was Heberer's Nasobame (*Tyrannonasus imperator*), which was quite a different animal. It had a poisonous claw at the tip of its tail, powerful rear legs to hold its prey, and sharply pointed teeth for ripping flesh from a victim.

The only defense the Morgenstern had against the Heberer was its tail. When the Heberer attacked, the Morgenstern wrapped its tail around a tree limb and swung back and forth and around and around, just out of the enemy's reach. As the Heberer followed the Morgenstern around and around, it soon became dizzy and threw up. This gave the Morgenstern the chance it needed to escape.

PIPE ORGAN TASSELSNOUTER (*Rhinochilopus musicus*). This species was five to seven feet long, perhaps the largest and possibly the most intelligent of all the snouters. It had nineteen pairs of snouts. It used the front-most pair as antennae and the eighteen remaining pairs as legs.

The male of this species was best known for its natural pipe organ. When not in use, it lay hidden under the skin of one of its cheeks. During the mating season, the tasselsnouter inflated its pipe organ to the size of a young boy's head. It then used its eighteen pairs of leg snouts as wind instruments, playing them by breathing first through one pair, then through another, and so on.

(*52*)

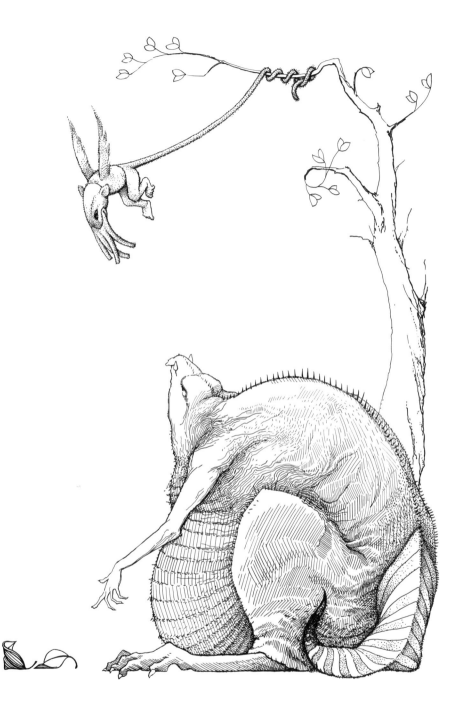

At first, it might make a series of mooing sounds, like those of a cow. Then it would give these mooing sounds at a higher pitch and a faster beat, until they became a thrumming sound, like that of a guitar played rapidly. At times, it added a sharp trembling sound of the kind a goat or sheep might make.

At the time of the year when day and night are of equal length, male tasselsnouters came together to play their pipe organs. It was the only time they did so. Meanwhile, their female friends moved slowly around them in a circle.

Petterssen-Skämtkvist managed to tame a male tasselsnouter during the years he spent on Hiduddify. He taught it to play two pieces of music for the organ by Johann Sebastian Bach.

After several years of study, Harald Stümpke and the other scientists at the Darwin Institute were almost ready to issue their report on snouters. However, Stümpke first went to Germany to meet with a zoologist named Gerolf Steiner. Steiner was going to make drawings of various snouters for the report. To help with the illustrations, Stümpke gave Steiner a summary of the report, as well as rough sketches of the snouters, and specimens of some living snouters. After several weeks, he returned to Hy-yi-yi, taking the specimens with him.

But, soon after he arrived, disaster struck. A secret underwater atomic test was carried out 125 miles to the east. A few minutes after the explosion occurred, the Hy-yi-yi Islands sank into the ocean and disappeared. Professor Dr. Stümpke, the scientists who worked with him, the records of their research, and all of the snouters on earth were lost.

Fortunately, Gerolf Steiner had the summary of the research that Stümpke had left with him. He also had the drawings he had made of the snouters from Stümpke's specimens. With this, he prepared the small book mentioned earlier. It is the only account we now have of these marvelous creatures and their vanished world.

But soon after the book was published, Professor Steiner admitted that he had made up the whole thing. There was no Hy-yi-yi, no Professor Dr. Harald Stümpke, and no snouters. They lived only in his imagination, and now, of course, in ours.

# Dream Bread

THREE boys were on a hiking trip, but they had not planned very well. When they pitched their tent the first night, they found they had nothing left to eat except a small piece of bread.

"If we divide the bread three ways," one of them said, "there will not be enough for all of us. And eating a tiny piece would only make us hungry for more."

"Let's skip supper and go to bed," the second one said. "The one who has the best dream can have all of it in the morning." The others agreed, and they crawled into the tent and went to sleep.

The next morning, each told about his dream. The first said he had dreamed that an angel was taking him up a golden staircase to heaven. At the top of the stairs, a golden door was open, and inside the door several angels were waiting for him.

The second one said he dreamed he had gone to an elegant feast. He ate and ate and ate until he thought he would burst.

The third one said that in his dream he had seen the other two. "When I saw you and the angel walking up the golden

staircase," he said to the first, "I was sure you would not be coming back. And when I saw *you* stuffing yourself," he said to the second, "I knew that you would not be hungry again for quite a while. So, in my dream, I came back here and ate the bread."

When the other two heard this, they rushed to their knapsacks and looked inside. It was true. The bread was gone. Not even a crumb was left.

# A Broomstick Trick

S AM said he could make a drinking glass filled with water stick to the ceiling.

"I've never seen that," said Henry.

"Nothing to it," said Sam. "It's just knowing how. I'll show you."

Sam filled a drinking glass with water, then stood up on a chair, and pressed the glass firmly against the ceiling. "It takes a little while for it to form a bond and stick," he said.

After a few minutes, Sam said his arm was getting tired. "Maybe you could hold this for me for a while," he said to Henry. "Better yet, get a broomstick from the kitchen."

When Henry came back with the broomstick, Sam told him to press it against the bottom of the glass. That would hold the glass in place, he said. When Henry got the stick in position, Sam let go of the glass and climbed down from the chair.

He started rubbing his arm. "That feels good," he said. "Well, thanks, Henry. See you later."

"Hey, when are you coming back?" Henry asked. "What do I do with the glass?" By then, the door had closed.

# The Great
# Dreadnought Hoax

IT was early in February 1910, in London. William Horace Cole was having lunch with a friend, a British naval officer aboard the *Dreadnought*, the world's mightiest battleship. His ship, along with much of the British fleet, was in port at Weymouth in the south of England.

Cole and the officer were discussing pranks and hoaxes. In recent years, Cole had become known as a clever prankster, and his friend was suggesting some trickery that caught his fancy.

"Why not pose as the emperor of someplace," he was saying, "and trick the Navy into giving you a guided tour of the *Dreadnought*. That would be something."

That night, Cole and his friend Adrian Stephen decided to do just that. Kings, sultans, emperors, and other leaders of tiny countries all over the world visited the fleet in a steady stream. With their hoax, they would show what nonsense these visits really were.

*(60)*

In the plan they worked out, the Emperor of Abyssinia and his three sons, the royal princes of Abyssinia (now Ethiopia), would visit the *Dreadnought*. Cole would impersonate "Herbert Cholmondelay" of the British Foreign Office, who was in charge of showing the Abyssinians around. Adrian would be "Herr Kauffmann," a German who was the official translator for the visitors.

The hoax was complicated and risky. As a result, it took them a while to find the four persons they needed to play the emperor and the princes. Everyone they asked was afraid of being arrested or being thrown overboard by some angry sailor.

Finally, they talked some of their friends into helping them. An athlete named Anthony Buxton agreed to pose as the Emperor of Abyssinia. Duncan Grant, an artist, and Gus Ridley, who was not working at the time, agreed to impersonate two of the royal princes. When no one else could be found to play the third prince, Virginia Stephen, Adrian's younger sister, agreed to do so.*

At the moment, there seemed to be only one remaining problem. The executive officer of the *Dreadnought* turned out to be a cousin of Adrian and Virginia's named Willy Fisher. Since Adrian was six feet five inches tall in his socks, he usually attracted some attention. He would be disguised, of course. But would Willy recognize him and ruin everything? They decided to go ahead and trust to good luck.

---

*A few years later, Virginia Stephen married and became Virginia Woolf, who, still later, became a famous novelist.

Cole learned that February 10 was the *Dreadnought's* fourth birthday. That was the ideal day for their hoax, he decided.

The first thing that morning, Cole sent a telegram to the Admiral of the Fleet at Weymouth, telling him to prepare for the arrival of the Emperor of Abyssinia and his royal party. He signed the telegram "Hardinge," the name of the man who headed the British Foreign Office.

Then he hurried to the Stephens' home in Fitzroy Square, where the tricksters were to meet. Three men from a costume firm were there with the clothing they needed. After they helped the Abyssinians to dress, they darkened their hands and faces and glued on black beards and mustaches.

The Abyssinians were not to eat or drink anything, they warned, or they would ruin their disguises. Unfortunately, none of them had eaten any breakfast.

For his role as Herr Kauffmann, the costumers turned Adrian's face a beefy-red color and added a brown mustache and beard and a bowler hat. As a member of the Foreign Office, all Cole needed was a top hat and a tailcoat.

At eight-thirty, the six impostors boarded a train at Paddington Station in London for the two-and-a-half-hour journey to Weymouth. They rode together in a private compartment. But when breakfast was served in the dining car, Cole and Adrian went off to eat and left the hungry Abyssinians on their own.

Needless to say, the two were nervous about what lay ahead. They worried about all sorts of things that might go wrong. Would the admiral's staff ignore the telegram, since it was not in a Foreign Office code? Would the Navy double-check with the Foreign Office? Would Cole be arrested for using Hardinge's name in the telegram? Would anyone meet their train? Would Willy Fisher see through their disguises and recognize his cousins Adrian and Virginia? If so, what would happen then?

When Cole and Adrian finally returned to their compartment, the Abyssinians threatened to revolt unless they were given something to eat. Cole brought each of them a bun, then watched closely while they chewed, for any damage to their makeup.

When the train pulled into the station at Weymouth, they breathed a sigh of relief. There waiting for them on the platform was a naval officer in full dress. He quickly came to their compartment and saluted the "emperor." In his role as Herbert Cholmondelay of the Foreign Office, Cole introduced the emperor, the royal princes, and Herr Kauffmann, the translator. The hoax had begun.

They were led along a red carpet, which had been rolled out in their honor, to a group of taxicabs, which took them to the harbor. There they boarded the admiral's personal launch, which took them out to the fleet.

As they approached the *Dreadnought*, they could see colorful flags flying from the masts and lines of British marines drawn up on the deck. Waiting for them were the Admiral of the Fleet, the captain of the *Dreadnought*, Cousin Willy Fisher, and other officers, all dressed in elegant white-and-gold uniforms.

Cholmondelay led the royal party aboard and introduced

each as he arrived on deck. Adrian found himself standing just a few yards from his cousin Willy. He was certain that Willy was staring at him. When Adrian saw the captain of the *Dreadnought*, he realized that he knew him personally, too.

They were members of the same club! They had taken walks
together! But when Adrian was introduced as Herr Kauffmann, they did not seem to recognize him.

The Abyssinians were asked to inspect a guard of honor.

The Admiral of the Fleet then began to rattle off a stream of facts and figures about the *Dreadnought*. Since the royal party was not supposed to speak English, Herr Kauffmann began to "translate" for them what the admiral was saying.

In preparing for the hoax, Adrian had tried to learn some Abyssinian, but it turned out to be too difficult. Instead, he memorized some snatches of Swahili, another language spoken in East Africa. In translating the admiral's words, he started with his Swahili. When he ran out of that, he began using passages of Latin and Greek he had learned as a boy. To make sure that these were not recognized, Adrian broke them up and mispronounced them.

The emperor and the princes had no idea what he was saying. But they would repeat some of it, and add some gibberish of their own. Adrian then told the admiral what he thought he wanted to know.

One of the officers commented on what an odd language Abyssinian seemed to be. He then said that a member of the *Dreadnought*'s crew spoke Abyssinian fluently. When the impostors heard that, they all felt a chill of fear. This was something they had not expected. But the officer then added, "Unfortunately, he is on leave."

After the royal party talked with the admiral, the captain took them on a tour of the ship. When it started to rain, Cole began to worry about their makeup. He was sure that it would be ruined or that the beards and mustaches would come loose. When he saw the emperor's mustache begin peeling off, he quickly suggested to the captain that they tour below deck, since the Abyssinians were not used to such weather. On the way down to the engine room, Cole managed to press the mustache back into place.

When they were offered lunch, the emperor and the princes all smiled broadly at the thought of eating at last. But Cole was afraid that eating also would ruin their disguises. He told the officers that the Abyssinians could not accept their invitation. Because of their religious beliefs, they could only eat food prepared in a special way.

By the time it stopped raining, the visit was drawing to a close. Soon, the impostors were in the admiral's personal launch on their way back to shore.

# WHO?

IF Princeton University only paid more attention to the little things in life—the date on which a person was born, for example, or how he pronounced his name—they would admit fewer students who do not exist.

Take the case of Joseph David Oznot of East Lansing, Michigan, the son of William H. Oznot, a wealthy private detective. He was one of 4,900 students who applied to Princeton in a recent year and one of 1,165 who were admitted.

Joseph's application for admission said he was first in his high-school class, a Latin student, a member of the varsity lacrosse team, class treasurer, a concert pianist, and, during the summers, a clerk in a hardware store. The recommendations from his teachers were wonderful. And his scores on the College Board entrance examinations were almost perfect.

When he visited Princeton for an interview, he arrived carrying the poems, in Latin, of the Roman poet Vergil and the latest issue of *Sports Illustrated*.

In the letter of acceptance Joseph received, the director of admissions at the university called him "an unusually gifted student." But Joseph was not just one student, he was six.

Two sophomores at Princeton had taken the College Board examinations in his name, and two had handled other details. A student at Columbia University had posed as Joseph at his interview, and a student at Michigan State University had provided him with a home address, fake high-school transcript, and recommendations from make-believe teachers.

But the director of admissions should have known that Joseph was a fake. If only he had noticed that his birthday was April Fools' Day, or if he had tried to pronounce "Oznot," which rhymes with "was not," or if he had examined his father's name and initials: William H. Oznot . . . W. H. O. . . . *WHO?*

# The Box Marked SECRET

SAMUEL R. Smith was the president of a bank and the owner of a coffin factory and an undertaking parlor. He was the richest man in town, but he also was a gloomy grouch who never laughed.

When he died, the will he left was as businesslike and gloomy as he was. But there was one clause that nobody fully understood. It read as follows:

"In the closet of my bedroom, you will find a large box that is wrapped in brown paper, sealed with wax, and marked SECRET. That box is not to be opened.

"The night after my funeral, my sons and lawyers will remove the box from the closet and carry it, wrapped and sealed, to the lawn behind my house. There they will make a fire, place the box in the flames, and see to it that it burns to ashes."

Smith's sons and lawyers did just what he asked. They moved the box to the back lawn. They built a roaring bonfire and placed the box in the flames.

Out of respect for Smith, none of them mentioned what they thought the box might contain. Silently, they watched it burn, each alone with his thoughts.

Then suddenly the box blew apart—and the sky filled
with fireworks.

(72)

# Lirpa Loof!

APRIL Fools' Day is not even mentioned on most calendars, since it is not an official holiday. Nor is much written or said about it. But somehow we all know when it arrives. Year after year, most people save at least some of their trickery for this day.

Perhaps the arrival of spring is a reminder. With the improvement in the weather, people are livelier, friskier, more playful, and trickier than usual. And their tricks are as simple and frothy as can be and take almost no time at all.

· They write KISS ME in big, bright letters on a piece of paper, and pin the paper to the back of someone's clothing without their knowing it.

· They glue a coin to a picnic table or to the sidewalk. Then they ask whose coin it is and watch the struggle as someone tries to pick it up.

· They send someone to the store for six buttonholes, or a stick with one end, or a bottle stretcher, or a packet of bumblebee feathers, or some freshly picked spaghetti noodles, or a history of Eve's grandmother, or whatever else they need.

· With a pin, they make a hole in the top of an egg, and

another at the bottom, through which they drain the white and the yolk. If someone eats a boiled egg for breakfast or packs one with his lunch, they substitute the eggshell for that. Or they make believe they are angry and throw the eggshell at someone, and watch the reaction.

Needless to say, you should be aware of these tricks and all the others, for someone might try one on you. Avoid eating chocolate-covered candies, for example, for they could be filled with cotton. And beware of pancakes anyone offers you. It is sad but true that on this day some mothers and fathers fill their pancakes with slightly smaller circles of cloth that cannot be seen—or chewed.

This kind of trickery goes on in many countries in this season. Often, it takes place not on April Fools' Day but on All Fools' Day, and there are other differences.

In France, an April fool is called an "April fish," *un poisson d'avril*, possibly because some fish are easier to catch at this time of year.

In Scotland, an April fool is a "gowk," the name the Scots use for cuckoo. April Fools' Day is Huntigowk Day, after an old Scottish prank played at this time of year. The victim is asked to deliver a letter to someone. When that person opens it, this message is inside.

*Don't laugh and don't smile,*
*Send the gowk another mile.*

The letter is resealed, and the gowk is told to deliver it to someone else. When delivery is made, that person sends the gowk to still another address. And so it goes, until it dawns on the messenger that he or she is being fooled.

In Mexico, All Fools' Day, or *Los santos inocentes*, is quite a different matter. It is observed December 28. On that day, anything anyone borrows does not have to be returned. Instead, the borrower sends a box of candy, a toy, or some other gift with a note reminding the lender that he or she has been fooled.

In India, the day is observed March 31 as the last day of the fertility festival of Huli or Holi. In other places, it is, of course, April 1. In Germany and Norway, it is observed twice, on April 1 *and* April 30.

No matter how much you know about April fooling, or how much experience you have had in trickery, there is a *very* good chance that in this season someone will manage to trick you in some way. But there is a bright side to this. You will have learned a new trick you now can try on someone else.

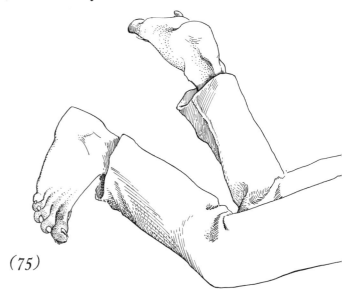

(75)

# Notes

The publications cited are described in the Bibliography.

THE CASE OF THE ROYAL ARABIAN JEWELS (p. 23). When the crown prince of Saudi Arabia (alias Jim Moran) spilled a case of fake jewels on a dance floor in Hollywood, it was not the first time that such a trick had been tried.

The trickster Hugh Troy was said to have bought large quantities of fake jewels at several five-and-ten-cent stores, then to have spent hours selecting the ones that looked the most like diamonds, emeralds, and rubies. He packed them in an old suitcase and carried it down Fifth Avenue, where, in front of a world-famous jeweler's (Tiffany's or Cartier's), the suitcase fell open, and out poured the fakes all over the sidewalk. It took police a half hour to get things back to normal. See Cerf, pp. 62–63.

GETTING OLDER AND OLDER FASTER AND FASTER (p. 33). The idea that a child can become as old as its father while they both are alive is, of course, nonsense. In the case described, there always will be thirty years between father and daughter, no matter how old they become. If both were several hundred years old, however, the difference would mean far less than it does in normal situations. See Barnum, pp. 145–47.

THE DAHUT (p. 34). This hoax on "greenhorns" is known not only in France but in its former possessions in North Africa. It also is known principally in rural areas of the United States and

Canada. But in the 1930s and 1940s it provided an introduction to life in the wilds for children attending summer camps in the Eastern United States.

In France, the greenhorn hunts a "dahut," which might be a bird or several kinds of animals, depending on the region. In the region of Brittany, it is said to resemble the side-hill gouger, one of the best-known of the American fearsome critters. In the region of Lorraine, it looks more like a small bear. In the United States and Canada, the prey is a snipe, a long-billed bird. If any of these animals is sighted, it can be trapped in a large sack. See Chartois; Randolph, *Church House*, pp. 40–42; Johana Smith; Schwartz, *Kickle Snifters*, pp. 32–33.

PIERRE BRASSAU (p. 46). There have been several hoaxes that tried to show that art critics who admire modern paintings may be unreliable in judging such work. One of the most successful involved a writer named Paul Jordon Smith who posed from 1924 to 1927 as a Russian artist named Pavel Jerdanovitch. Smith began his hoax when portraits by his wife, Sarah Bixby Smith, a professional portrait artist, were criticized for not being "modern" enough.

Although Smith had never painted before, he borrowed from his wife some old tubes of paint, an old brush, and some canvases, and with several quick, savage strokes of the brush created a sketch of a South Pacific native holding up a starfish. Since the starfish actually turned out more like a banana, he called the painting "Yes, We Have No Bananas."

When Smith entered his creation in a French art show, he changed its name to "Exaltation," which he felt sounded more "artistic." After the painting was praised by critics, he did several others as quickly as the first. He gave them names such as "Aspiration" and "Illumination" and entered them in important shows. Again and again, critics praised him as an artist who was breaking new ground. When he finally revealed his hoax, the story traveled around the world. See MacDougall, pp. 267–68.

SNOUTERS (p. 48). Snouters are but one family among a great many remarkable creatures that never drew breath. These range from dragons, basilisks, and sea serpents of old to animals concocted more recently, like kickle snifters, lufferlangs, and squonks, to fake animals that could actually be seen and touched, including mermaids, a winged cat, a pygmy bison, and a fur-bearing trout. See Schwartz, *Kickle Snifters*; Dance.

A BROOMSTICK TRICK (p. 58). This parlor trick was reported in an ancient tale, but in a different guise. Instead of a drinking glass, a man seems to be holding a giant rock in place so that it does not roll down a hill. Or he appears to be holding up the roof of a porch or a house.

A traveler sees him and asks what he is doing. He explains that the rock will roll or that the roof will fall. He then asks the simpleton to help him. There is an emergency at home. Would he take his place for just a few minutes until he returns? In some versions, he borrows the dupe's horse so that he can get home and return even faster. But he doesn't return. Finally, the traveler realizes that he has been tricked.

In some versions, the trickster is holding a hat on the ground. He tells the traveler that it covers a rare bird or a treasure of some sort, and he must leave for a few minutes to get a cage for the bird or a chest for the treasure. When the trickster does not return, the traveler lifts the hat and finds nothing, or some animal dung. See Thompson, p. 202.

THE GREAT DREADNOUGHT HOAX (p. 60). A week after the hoax took place, a detailed story about it appeared in the *London Daily Mail*, along with the picture the tricksters had taken of themselves the morning they set out. There even were references in the story to the shouts of "Bunga! Bunga!" by the Abyssinians when they were shown the *Dreadnought*'s big guns. William Cole admitted that he had leaked the story to the press. It was too good a secret to keep, he said.

The expression "Bunga! Bunga!" soon became a faddish catchword in everyday conversation in England. It also began to appear in jokes and songs performed at vaudeville shows. In addition, whenever the *Dreadnought*'s officers went ashore, they were heckled by children who followed them, shouting, "Bunga! Bunga!"

The House of Commons and the Royal Navy began separate investigations of the hoax. One concern was how the hoaxers had managed to arrange a visit so easily. Another involved the usefulness of the general practice of entertaining foreign officials aboard British warships.

There was one other result. The Stephens' cousin Willy Fisher took steps to "avenge the honor of the Royal Navy." Fisher and other officers from the *Dreadnought* "punished" William Cole and Duncan Grant, one of the royal princes, with a symbolic caning, lightly striking each across his bottom several times with a cane. See Stephen, pp. 34–46; Saunders, pp. 73–79.

LIRPA LOOF! (p. 73). Although the tradition of April fooling is widespread, no one is certain how it began. Many beginnings have been suggested, including these:

The ancient Hindu fertility festival of Huli in India, which is marked by high spirits, bonfires, and dancing. When it concludes on March 31, the unsuspecting are sent on fool's errands.

The adoption of a new calendar in France in 1564, which changed the celebration of New Year's Day from April 1 to January 1. April 1 had been a time for the exchange of visits and gifts. The many who continued to celebrate on that day became the targets of jokes and tricks. They received fake invitations to parties and mock visits and gifts.

Various celebrations which marked the vernal equinox and the arrival of spring in the Northern Hemisphere suggested two other possibilities. The uncertainty of the weather in that season led to a belief that nature was playing tricks and providing humans with an example to follow. The general improvement in the weather at that time was a source of playful feelings which also encouraged April fooling. See Leach, *Dictionary*, "April Fool's Day"; "April First"; Hatch, pp. 314–16; Chambers, pp. 460–62.

# Sources

The sources of each item are given, along with variants and related information. Publications cited are described in the Bibliography.

*page* 3  *Bald-Headed Whizzers.* "Or he comes up behind," from Pat Larish, Cocalico School, near Lancaster, Pa., 1982.

5  *The Magic Turtle.* A tale known in the Ozark Mountains region of Arkansas and Missouri and also in France. Retold from Clough, pp. 665–66, quoting from Zinsser. For variants, Randolph, *Talking Turtle,* pp. 97–98; Smith, *Practical Joker,* pp. 195–96.

8  *. . . and the Shrinking Head.* Adapted from a practical joke in the oral tradition. Reference to the shrinking cane in the retelling, Smith, *Practical Joker,* p. 215.

11  *Onions.* A retelling of a story that appeared in the comic almanacs popular in the United States in the early nineteenth century. In this version, the hero is Israel Putnam, an American Revolutionary War general who had a reputation for a wry sense of humor. Rourke, p. 115.

13  *Rattlesnake Soup.* Adapted and retold from Rollins, *Gone Haywire,* pp. 31–36.

15  *Johnny Chung and the Flying Figments.* Retold from information in Adams; "Plainfield Teachers"; *Time*; Saunders, pp. 103–8.

19  *The Organ That Brayed Like a Donkey.* Adapted and retold from Smith, *Practical Joker,* pp. 121, 123–27; MacDougall, p. 40.

23  *The Case of the Royal Arabian Jewels.* Adapted and retold from Smith, *Practical Joker,* pp. 142–43.

25  *Footprints on the Ceiling.* Adapted from Sandburg, p. 40.

26  *"A Nude Horse . . ."* Adapted and retold from information in

*page*     Abel; "Playboy after Hours"; Saunders, pp. 32–46; Draper, "Crusade Against Naked Animals"; "SINA Introduces Campus to Clothed Animals"; collector's correspondence with Abel, 1983.

33   *Getting Older and Older* . . . A puzzle in the oral tradition.

34   *The Dahut.* Adapted and retold from Chartois; Randolph, *Church House*, pp. 40–42; Johana Smith.

38   *The Wonderful Horse.* Based on a fourteenth-century jest from the German trickster Till Eulenspiegel. Adapted and retold from Clouston, *Popular Tales and Fictions*, pp. 52–53. There is also an English nursery rhyme on the subject: "There was a sight near Charing Cross, / A Creature almost like a Horse; / But when I came this Beast to see, / The Head was where the Tail should be." See Opie, *Nursery Rhymes*, #467, pp. 379–80.

40   *Alex and Avery.* Adapted and retold from Smith, *Practical Joker*, p. 180.

42   *Billy the Milkmaid.* Adapted and retold from Benton, pp. 189–92.

46   *Pierre Brassau.* Retold from information in "Zoo Story"; Saunders, pp. 191–92.

48   *Snouters.* Based on Stümpke; Dance, pp. 119–21; Lyons.

56   *Dream Bread.* A tale traced to at least the third century B.C. in Persia (now Iran). Adapted from variants in Clouston, *Popular Tales*, pp. 86–98, and Baum, pp. 378–79, 400–5. Variants have also been found in such diverse sources as a Buddhist sacred book, the ancient *Book of Sindibad*, and European jest books. Modern versions have been collected in French Canada, Nova Scotia, and Maine, and in the Sea Islands of South Carolina. See Parsons, pp. 68–69; Fauset, p. 54.

58   *A Broomstick Trick.* Adapted from a traditional parlor trick. See Leach, *Riddle Me*, pp. 109–10; Thompson, p. 202.

60   *The Great Dreadnought Hoax.* A retelling based on information in Stephen; Hone, pp. 155–70; Saunders, pp. 61–79.

68   *WHO?* Retold from information in the articles "Princeton Accepts Sophomores' Hoax," "How to Get into Princeton."

71   *The Box Marked SECRET.* Adapted and retold from Smith, *Practical Joker*, p. 55.

73   *Lirpa Loof!* Chambers, pp. 460–62; Hatch, pp. 314–16; "April First"; Leach, "April Fool's Day," *Dictionary*, pp. 36–37; "With a pin . . . ," collected at Mabel Baron School, Stockton, Calif., 1979.

# Bibliography

## Books

Books that may be of interest to young people are marked with an asterisk (*).

Abel, Alan. *The Great American Hoax*. New York: Trident Press, 1966.

Barnum, P. T. *Struggles and Triumphs, or the Life of P. T. Barnum, Written by Himself*, Vol. 1. George S. Bryan, ed. New York: Alfred A. Knopf, 1927.

Benton, Jesse James. *Cow by the Tail*. Boston: Houghton Mifflin, 1943.

Botkin, B. A. *A Treasury of American Folklore*. New York: Crown, 1944.

Cerf, Bennett. *Shake Well Before Using—A New Collection of Impressions and Anecdotes, Mostly Humorous*. New York: Simon and Schuster, 1948.

Chambers, Robert, ed. *A Miscellany of Popular Antiquities*, Vol. 1. London: W. & R. Chambers, 1886.

Clough, Ben C. *The American Imagination at Work*. New York: Alfred A. Knopf, 1947.

Clouston, W. A. *The Book of Noodles*, Vol. 2. London: Elliott Stock, 1888.

———. *Popular Tales and Fictions*. Edinburgh, Scotland: William Black and Sons, 1882.

Cullin, Mollie. "The Fabulous Lester Green." As quoted in Clough, above.

Dance, Peter. *Animal Fakes & Frauds*. Maidenhead, Berkshire, England: Sampson Low, 1976.

Eastman, Max. *Enjoyment of Laughter*. New York: Simon and Schuster, 1936.

Fauset, Arthur Hull. *Folklore from Nova Scotia*. New York: Memoirs of the American Folklore Society, 1931.

Hatch, Jane M., ed. *The American Book of Days*, 3d ed. New York: H. W. Wilson Company, 1978.

Hone, Joseph M. "The Abyssinian Princes Who Outwitted the British Navy," in Alexander Klein, ed., *Grand Deception*, pp. 166–70. New York: J. B. Lippincott, 1955.

Leach, Maria, ed., "April Fool's Day," in *Standard Dictionary of Folklore, Mythology and Legend*. New York: Funk & Wagnalls Publishing Co., 1972.

———. *Riddle Me, Riddle Me, Ree*. New York: The Viking Press, 1970.

Leitch, Alexander. *A Princeton Companion*. Princeton, N.J.: Princeton University Press, 1978.

MacDougall, Curtis D. *Hoaxes*. New York: Macmillan, 1940. Reprinted New York: Dover Publications, 1958.

Opie, Iona and Peter. *The Lore and Language of Schoolchildren*. London: Oxford University Press, 1959.

———. *The Oxford Dictionary of Nursery Rhymes*. Oxford, England: Clarendon Press, 1951.

Parsons, Elsie Clews. *Folk-Lore of the Sea Islands, South Carolina*. New York: Memoirs of the American Folklore Society, 1923.

Randolph, Vance. *The Talking Turtle and Other Ozark Folk Tales*. New York: Columbia University Press, 1957.

———. *Who Blowed Up the Church House? And Other Ozark Folk Tales*. New York: Columbia University Press, 1952.

Rollins, Philip A. *The Cowboy*. New York: Charles Scribner's Sons, 1922.

*———. *Gone Haywire: Two Tenderfeet on the Montana Range in 1886*. New York: Charles Scribner's Sons, 1939.

Rourke, Constance. *American Humor: A Study of the National Character*. New York: Harcourt, Brace & Co., 1931.

Sandburg, Carl. *The Prairie Years*. New York: Harcourt, Brace & Co., 1926. Reprinted as *Abraham Lincoln: The Prairie Years and the War Years*, Vol. 1. New York: Dell, 1960.

Saunders, Richard. *The World's Greatest Hoaxes*. New York: Playboy Press, 1980.

* Schwartz, Alvin. *Kickle Snifters and Other Fearsome Critters*. New York: J. B. Lippincott, 1976.

*———. *Whoppers: Tall Tales and Other Lies*. New York: J. B. Lippincott, 1975.

*———. *Flapdoodle: Pure Nonsense from American Folklore*. New York: J. B. Lippincott, 1980. Includes catches.

# BIBLIOGRAPHY

* ————. *Tomfoolery: Trickery and Foolery with Words.* New York: J. B. Lippincott, 1973. Includes catches.

Smith, H. Allen. *The Compleat Practical Joker.* New York: Doubleday, 1953. Reprinted New York: William Morrow, 1980.

Stephen, Adrian. *The Dreadnought Hoax.* London: The Hogarth Press, 1936.

Stümpke, Harald (Gerolf Steiner). *The Snouters: Form and Life of the Rhinogrades.* New York: The Natural History Press, 1967.

Thompson, Stith. *The Folktale.* New York: Holt, Rinehart and Winston, 1946. Reprinted Berkeley, Calif.: University of California Press, 1977.

Toor, Frances. *A Treasury of Mexican Folkways.* New York: Crown, 1967.

Wright, Lawrence. *Clean and Decent: The Fascinating History of the Bathroom and the Water Closet.* Toronto: University of Toronto Press, 1967.

Zinsser, Hans. *As I Remember Him: The Biography of R.S.* Boston: Little, Brown; Atlantic Monthly Press, 1940.

## *Periodicals*

Adams, Caswell. "Brokers Find Phantom School Easy Issue to Sell in Football," New York *Herald Tribune,* Nov. 14, 1941, p. 30. Account of Plainfield Teachers football hoax.

"April First," *Western Folklore* 8 (1949): 270.

Baum, Paull F. "The Three Dreams or 'Dream Bread' Story," *Journal of American Folklore* 30 (1917): 378–410.

Chartois, Jo. "Hunting the Dahut: A French Folk Custom," *Journal of American Folklore* 58 (1945): 21–24. Account of a hunting hoax similar to a snipe hunt.

Draper, George. "Crusade Against Naked Animals," *San Francisco Chronicle,* Aug. 13, 1962, p. 1. Account of the animal clothing hoax.

————. "City Called 'Moral Disaster Area,'" *San Francisco Chronicle,* Aug. 14, 1962, p. 1.

————. "The Zoo Shocks a Crusader," *San Francisco Chronicle,* Aug. 15, 1962, p. 1.

————. "'Solution' on Naked Animals," *San Francisco Chronicle,* Aug. 16, 1962, p. 1.

"How to Get into Princeton," *Time,* April 24, 1964, p. 71. Phantom applicant is admitted.

# BIBLIOGRAPHY

Loomis, C. Grant. "Some Folklore of Yankee Genius," *Western Folklore* 6 (1947): 341–49.

Lyons, Richard D. "The Origin of a Fabulous Species," *The New York Times*, May 17, 1967, p. 1. Account of the snouter hoax.

Passarga, Eberhard. Letter to editor regarding Snouter hoax, *Natural History* 67 (Aug. 1967): 82.

"Plainfield Teachers." *The New Yorker*, Nov. 29, 1941, pp. 16–17.

"Playboy after Hours," *Playboy*, Sept. 1963, p. 10. Account of the animal clothing hoax.

"Princeton Accepts Sophomores' Hoax for Class of '68," *The New York Times*, April 18, 1964, p. 31.

"SINA Introduces Campus to Clothed Animals," *Daily Californian*, University of California at Berkeley, Dec. 3, 1962, p. 1.

Smith, Johana H. "In the Bag: A Study of Snipe Hunting," *Western Folklore* 16 (1957): 107–10.

Stümpke, Harald (Gerolf Steiner). "The Snouters," *Natural History* 67 (June 1967): 8–13.

*Time*, Nov. 17, 1941, p. 74. Plainfield Teachers football hoax is revealed in untitled article.

"Zoo Story," *Time*, Feb. 21, 1964, p. 71. Account of Pierre Brassau hoax.